When the Titans Sleep and Other Dreams

Poems by Patrick Dobson

Kansas City   Spartan Press   Missouri

Spartan Press

Kansas City, Missouri

spartanpresskc@gmail.com

Copyright (c) Patrick Dobson, 2018
First Edition 1 3 5 7 9 10 8 6 4 2
ISBN: 978-1-946642-87-5
LCCN: 2018964700

Design, edits and layout: Jason Ryberg
Cover and title page images: Patrick Dobson
Author photo: courtesy of Johnson County Community College
All rights reserved. No part of this publication may be
reproduced or transmitted in any form or by any means,
electronic or mechanical, including photocopying,
recording or by info retrieval system, without prior
written permission from the author.

Spartan Press would like to thank Prospero's Books, The Fellowship of N-finite Jest, The Prospero Institute of Disquieted P/o/e/t/i/c/s, Will Leathem, Tom Wayne, Jeanette Powers, j. d. tulloch, Jon Lee Grafton, Jason Preu, Mark McClane, Tony Hayden and the whole Osage Arts Community.

CONTENTS

first spring rain / 1

pruning makes me a good citizen / 2

March 29, 2017 / 3

spring on the avenida / 4

tulips / 5

when lilacs bloom / 6

rabbit, spring / 8

spring-fed pool / 9

Swimming, Swope Park, 1971 / 10

Sunset, June 22 / 11

Boy Scouts / 12

Drought / 13

Weed Trees / 14

Needles, California / 15

Tending the Rain Garden / 16

an end to the drought / 17

early freeze / 19

October / 20

snowman / 21

November 23 / 22

Sunday Walk / 23

salt / 25

snowman grows up / 26

Trier, 1986 / 27

down from billings / 28

leaving home / 31

sisters / 33

Files / 34

Six Feet from a Spider / 35

The Side Porch / 37

East Glacier Lake / 38

Sales Meeting, Redux / 39

Radio Flyer / 40

chopping wood / 41

Tight Blue / 42

The Lover / 43

every damn day / 44

dark / 46

filibuster / 48

Playhouse / 50

Ismael Gallegos, Superman / 51

Elizabeth Dobson, Oct. 7, 1903-April 3, 2001 / 52

Fighting Fires / 54

to walk / 56

Bum / 57

Against the End of Hope, or John Stack's
  Last Good Try / 58

The Buddha, 39th and Main / 59

Tamale Lady / 60

Tree Surgeon / 61

farm kid / 62

Home to Roost / 63

When the Titans Sleep / 64

family photo / 65

missouri / 66

sacrifice / 67

landscaping / 68

Night Terrors / 69

I Am This City / 71

highway beautification / 75

the retreat from al alamein / 77

Signals / 79

sales meeting / 80

apparitions / 81

alone no more / 82

surface tension / 83

out of shadow and light / 84

Price of Success / 85

epoch / 86

I dedicate this book to friend, thinker, and
philosopher Pat O'Kelley

first spring rain

a city rinsed and rinsed again
in two days worth of washboard rain

finally
the place is spring cleaned

curbs scoured, yards scrubbed
of three months of dog

tree trunks tidied
for new messages

pruning makes me a good citizen

I sawed and chopped.
Ruthless, I took everything
in the way of a good harvest.

My sheers bit the wood,
I tasted jam and cider,
pie and cobbler and sauce.

Pruning makes me a good citizen.
Low boughs gone, my neighbor
will stand erect when he mows his yard.

Children will have apples to share
as they pass my yard
on the way to the park.

Despite my work, I haven't
tamed that tree. It minds me not.
I take some to get more,

For a season, a year.
My tools will wear out
before that tree does.

March 29, 2017

The thunderstorm upset lawn furniture,
Showed the gutters clogged.
Electric eyes fooled, the streetlights blinked;
Drops the size of nickels.

The best storms rumble in over the river,
Ones that stall and rip through our chests.

The wind smells of new wheat and electricity,
Shocks that float in the windows
And settle on the armchair, waiting.

Hail begins and we worry over the roof.
In the hand, an ice rock casts halos
Across its jawbreaker core.

We put the stone in the freezer.
It seemed worth saving—
A reminder when we find it
Long after we've forgotten

That we lived through this one,
Our chests and roofs intact, whole.
We roll hail in our fingers.
And wait for news from the prairie.

spring on the avenida

I

starlings rise
like smoke in a cold city
cat claws the window

II

branches, skeletal stiff,
grow lithe, buds sprout overnight
wind, storm, lightning, hail

III

two chinese bakers
sit in bright, spring sun, eyes closed
fish in sparkling streams

tulips

seas of butterfly peas flutter;
purple, blue swollen petals unfold,
welcome light and warmth in the still of garden

apple blossoms fall soundless across broad shoulders,
cling to the gardener's sweater as she clips
jonquil, gladiola, from hordes of like blooms

a blanket cast in the tulip bed and lounged upon;
a gardner, fertile and strong, sunglowed, rounded, lithe,
smelling of earth and flower and mown grass

spirea caresses two bodies, sun-warm skin—
breath, mulch-soft and green-cool;
the tulips riot in a breeze, erupt in frenzies of joy

when lilacs bloom

we lost hope
winter seemed forever
spring so far away

we cowered inside
our faces turned from windows
hidden in blankets

while we looked away
frightened beyond all reason
that cold would surely end us

lilacs bloomed like surprises
whipped out of gardens
on winds through front doors

lilacs' aromas conjured horizons
where green wheat met stormy skies
thunder shook creation

then we knew again
lilacs smell better on days
sodden with rain and lightning flashes

tempests rip flowers
into still-cold spring
but gales can't harm them

they've reminded us
how far we have come
into the light

rabbit, spring

it sat under the lilac,
mouth busy with fescue and clover
this tiny bit of yard, claimed as our own,
free of predators

healthy, big, and brown
ears cocked my direction
with one cow-like eye
it watched me watch it

it knew, somehow, i'm sure
that five feet distant,
on the other side of the fence
hounds in pavolovian anticipation waited

we sat still, me in the car, it under the lilac
the urban world a-buzz
cars, air conditioners, sirens in the distance
mailbox full of obligatories

a breath of air
dreams of soft moments
quiet padded feet
neck and face relaxing

it was our moment
together
away from worries that dogged us

spring-fed pool

oak-shaded and pine-needled,
free raptor of claw,
iridescent crawdads jet through hairy algae

a school of madtoms futz around tea-brown decay
while a darter trio — two stippled and an orangethroat—
plot a run against the pumpkinseeds
lolling at the edge of the sapphire seep

a sculpin, the ancient old man, impatient
with the bluegill and shiner gossip
scuttles rock to rock
settles on the snapper's back

an eye moves with the sculpin
as it hovers up off the shell
and glides toward a stick-tip of a nose

Swimming, Swope Park, 1971

Picnic baskets spilled, sticky pop gone flat,
salty, soggy chips, peanutbuttermesses,
sunburn noses, jammed thumbs,
toes skinned on the bottom of the pool.

Chairs and towels, whining boys,
impatient sisters lost in parking lot reflections,
sun like murder.

But at the edge of the pool
a mother gazes at the waves,
water nymphs flash in her eyes.

Sunset, June 22

A long walk, enough
to stir the air in the schoolyard
and bring the cats home for milk.

The girl, new-whirled from the merry-go-round,
chatters ahead on the sidewalk,
waves her hands up at the cottonwoods
as if parting the waters.

The wind in the trees
sounds like a river.

Boy Scouts

In the meadow,
the cabin's tin roof rang out under rain
that came straight down, warm,
as we ran for the lone pin oak.

We sneered at lightning,
turned face and naked chest
to the deluge.

Frogs rolled out of the forest,
a sleepy plague. We plucked them
from the meadow and grass
stuck up between our toes

as if we had grown there.

Drought

Grass burns blond.
Tree leaves droop.
Old men douse azaleas with spouted cans.

Corn in the garden
dead a while now,
stands skeletal,
yellow, hard-cracked.

Three months in and hope is lost.
Cats have gone into hiding,
and dogs sag with tails
between their legs.

People rush home
through brown haze to huddle in.
Evening, a hush falls along sidestreets.
Tire swings sway empty.

Weed Trees

One elm, a cabal of invasive meanness,
spreads bombs that sprout
along the fence line and down under the wall.
These Siberian elms are going to kill me.
They grow out from under the lilacs.
The roses harbor their little saw-toothed leaves
until it's too late to stop them.

Left alone a season, they spring up
two feet or more, quaking before no man.
Chemicals and shears can't battle back
the onslaught — my crusades fruitless.
The elms flow in waves over the ramparts,
too many too fast. They back me into a corner
wild eyed, obsessed, overwrought.

One time, digging in the crawlspace
to make room for a new furnace,
I discovered the Siberian elm's secret.
Grabbling through the dirt, I uncovered
networks of wiry strands with pale sprouts
bursting from them. I can't beat a force
whose roots encircle the earth.

Needles, California

A hot place, four dried pines from ascension,
and willing to spread, like smoke,
heavenward.

People shimmer in mirages—
sticks quaking in sun
coming off all that trailer park chrome.

And dust, lots of dust,
chokes throats, chafes eyes,
makes noses bleed.

But it's good here, and quiet.
Especially at night. The cool settles,
even those pines seem alive.

Tending the Rain Garden

Dried stalks of big bluestem
reach six or more feet, form a jungle
that takes a weed whip and stamina
to get through.

My son, a 14 year old,
helped with the work,
hacked last year's growth
into stiff bundles.

We stacked the bluestem in brush piles
along with leaves and swamp willow branches
that gathered in the garden.
Another season of labor.

He stripped a stalk of its leaves
down to its stiff backbone.
Imagine, he said as he snapped it,
that this is what keeps a plant upright.

I watched him as he examined
plants one by one, learning their nature—
one spine just forming, another ossified,
barely keeping an old man standing.

an end to the drought

Guillermo José Guerra Carrillo
never complained about drought,
it will end, he said, it always does

the tequila never stopped,
and that was almost as good
as rain sweeping over the desert
breaking the monotony of sun and heat

one night, Memo sang about how he
and his Comanche kin rode with Pancho Villa,
picked their way across the sky islands,
and shot Texas Rangers for fun and sport

the revolution was good then,
he said, anything went—
a strapping woman with red hair and a winchester
squeezed him and his horse
until they fainted with delight

Pershing and his Army regulars,
Obregon's frumpy green men,
ran eyes wide, mouths agape, lungs bursting,
from Villa's Mexicans, Comanches,
and what was left of the Apaches

Memo and Villa's men waved their rifles like antennae,
and showed Pershing's Punitive Expedition
a modern war where fairness was a matter of opinion

cool wind sweeps up over Chihuahua tonight
over the gravestones on this bank
of the Rio Bravo del Norte
where Memo danced in the blond grass
with a jug of wine

rain falls with a sigh

early freeze

meteor streaks trap goldfish flutter
sadness frosts a fallen leaf—
an ice-skinned cherub leans frozen
in a tumble of sighs
draped on lost time

October

The season flitters into the corners of the house,
dust-laced and leaf-crumbed.
The dog brings in the cold on its back.

The light, suffused with yellow and red,
comes late, leaves early, bathes us all,
until into somnambulant trance we fall

and seek only sleep and food. And everything,
even the lovers we run our tongues over,
tastes of walnut husks and pine resin.

snowman

the morning sun decapitated
the snowman and smacked that smile
and button eyes right off his face

the dog chewed up his boots

the sun sets now,
his carrot nose lies in the grass,
his hat up near the door

on the end of a stick a glove waves goodbye

November 23

Evening light, sharp, malicious,
streaks winter across the porch.
It won't be long now;
our dreams will fill with sun.
We'll daydream of dogs in the park
and children on bicycles
beneath the canopy of oaks.

It's just so as long day
transforms into long night.
I see my breath, count the days,
hope that old men like me
have enough to keep them warm.

Evening light streaks winter across the porch,
my fire insignificant against the night.
Somewhere a boy's aching
to go outside without his jacket.

Inside the house,
a flower in the vase at the bay window
closes against the darkness.

Sunday Walk

(A meditation on Claude Monet's "View of Argenteuil, snow")

The wind died in the night,
leaving skeins of new snow and a hush
on every branch and fence.

Morning, we tread paths, crunch and swish,
as we make our way down from the rail station
and through the gardens
behind the houses along boulevard.
I hold your hand lightly, friendly,
wary of driving you away.

We nod to ladies strolling,
umbrellas opened against the snow,
men in dress shoes.
I didn't wear enough clothes,
my jacket is too light.
I can feel the heat of the stoves
in apartments sealed tight against the season.

Snowflakes cling to your dark skirt,
stars and comets gather at your feet.
Beyond, the factory dark and locked
waits for me under bleached sky,
its chimney a reminder tomorrow starts the week.

I squint and the cold catches in my throat.
We will have a coffee in the café
and warm ourselves by the stove.

We are quiet. I can hear your heartbeat.

salt

under burden of snow
the city grows quiet

human beings at work,
the only movement tonight

shovel scrape, crunch,
tires sing on icy pavement

breaths hang in streetlight,
mumbles, moans, and sighs

snow ends the business
of salvagers and gleaners

they join their fellows, shuffling,
citizens who have little to do

but sprinkle their labors with salt
and inhale the night

snowman grows up

the sun shown on the snow-day
when the children rolled, stacked,
hatted, dressed, and gloved him,

then, proud of their work
they took the sled to the hill
in the park and forgot him

when school opened again
and children were away
his carrot nose fell, point first

into the ball below his waist
and the snowman, grown up,
saluted age, maturity, and death

he was smiling, of course,
sun on his cheery cheeks
and button eyes

neighbors, friends, compatriots!
he seemed to say, *come and see*
the breath of life breathed into me

Trier, 1986

Through grape-heavy trellis,
we watched a city effervesce
on the river like dreaming.
We ran barefoot over smooth,
cool cobble stones,
drank wine in the sun.

The vines bloomed, hung with fruit,
were harvested, then pruned and tied.
Waiting for a new season,
the vineyard stood empty.
Snow covered steep paths and rows
above the city and the river.

Now, the cathedral bell tolls midnight,
echoes through mist on quiet streets.
The stream flows beneath ice
by the old mill as if you never left,
and years hadn't passed between us.

down from billings

*It was prophesied that Kronos, king of the gods, would lose his
throne to his son, just as he had taken rule from his own father.
To vacate the prophesy, Kronos swallowed his children at their
birth. But Rhea, his wife, saved one boy by giving Kronos a stone
to swallow instead and spiriting the redeemed boy to Crete.
As an adult, Zeus overthrew Kronos and imprisoned him on Tartaros
in a deep pit. Centuries later, Zeus had mercy on his father,
released him from his prison and put him on the throne of Elysium.*

back then,
he lifted his chin, profile with mountain teeth,
and breathed a breath, a little flit of a sound
quiet as butterfly wing

down the divide at the wheel of the dodge,
he grew louder—was heard in winds
that ratcheted along knuckly ridges,
white as bones

eyes afire, bow-strong in the shoulder,
arms like knotted rope, hands like blacksmith tongs
big enough to wrap my head, all and then,
as if banished, none

he knocked heads, kept his boys at bay,
decided he would commmand all
and throttle the world and the people in it
with his fists

mother saved us then, put us into back rooms.
cautioned us to walk on our toes,
and not say a word until the old man
settled asleep behind his whiskey

i ignored the old man;
when i matured and countered the world on my own,
i imprisoned him in his own home
where he had no one to command

it was then he felt impotence
he could move nothing in the world
but the channel on the television
and his bottle of bourbon

separated from my father,
i have seen the mountains again;
they aren't nearly as big,
their teeth not as sharp,
the air not as clear

and he's grown small,
frame crooked as an old door,
he limps, hair grayed, arms weak,
back bowed, he mumbles about weather,
his eyes dark and cold

we talk now and again,
his voice trembling, raspy
he tells me of the old days
but i remember them well
he was large then, bigger than any man

with a nod to his greatness
i give the phone to my son
who listens to the aged man's stories
and wonders what i'll be like
when i am old

leaving home

that summer, the park ached
with the screams and yips
of kids and dogs loosed
upon it

it was green then,
pool full, moms wearing sunglasses,
kids with flippers and sea-monster floats,
people burned weenies, took in a breeze,
smiled at each other
with beer-foam moustaches

around, in the houses, mamas sang in kitchens—
bread steam, meat-and-potato sear
floated over the baseball diamond
crawling with those spidery little guys
on St. Helena's B-Team
beating the pants off St. John Francis Regis again—
porches creaked, smoldered with cigars,
a hundred dogs on every block
raised the living and the dead
at each out-of-sync clock chime

anyone who had any money
bought grape pop in a bottle
a pack of luckies, or a snort of whiskey

that summer, in the park,
in the pool, we watched
young mamas and older sisters
cross and uncross their legs,
snap their swimsuit tops
and pull the elastic out from behind
with index fingers

it was before life became knotty,
before the girls got pregnant,
and things went bad with cops
parents, brothers and sisters

and we all got the hell out

that summer was as good
as it was ever going to get
but there was no way to trace the lines
through the waves in the water,
to see our reflections in the sunglasses

sisters

back then, when the hills were too big,
we walked our bikes to fire hydrant rest stops
where we ate tomatoes we swiped from
Everly's garden, apples from Old Man Cole's and
strawberries, hot and sweet, off the pyramid beneath

back home, we waited until hot garden-hose water
ran cold, our bare feet in cool grass
then, we scrambled for the corner of the house
to formulate a lie, make up another story
much the same as the last

it's funny to remember how good
stolen fruit tastes when it's eaten under hot sun,
bikes propped against our knees,
and the way hose water quenched thirst so well
once it ran cold—

and sad to see we're still hiding
in the bushes from the man
in the back door

Files

If I were to die today,
my executors would go to folders
hung in a stainless-steel rack with wheels
I use to shuffle around
the accretions of living.

Lonely, the files swing in the basement.
Receipts, life and home insurance,
taxes paid and due, passports,
the mortgage payment schedule.
The folders' contents see daylight
but once a quarter or year
or just the one time.

They are the last and final snapshot
of a life amortized.
Interest decreases, equity increases
until I finally balance
and wraiths gather in the park
to spread my ashes.

Six Feet from a Spider

When I was a kid,
a lady next door panicked
when she found spiders
in her bouffant.

I itched all over when I discovered
she combed her do just
once in a month at
a hairdresser down the street.

The arachnids weren't the problem.

The spiders above my desk
have been busy all these years.
Successions of webs,
some heavy with dust, age tattered,
undulate as the furnace kicks on.

How many? These little creatures
covered the lampshade
and books along the shelf.
Webs, orb and cob, indicate
three or four different kinds,
excluding jumping spiders
who make no frail weaves
to float on air currents.

I favor spiders,
understand their work,
love their magical arts.
Hermits doing good,
they arrived without an invite,
infested these joists,
devoured the other uninvited.

They have saved me from legions
of indecent wickedness.

Leave these webs alone, I say.
I take comfort in the work
spiders do for us sinners.
But for them, my world suffers.

I like to believe a myth
and dream in my sleep:
Like that lady long ago,
wherever I roam
I'm no farther than six feet
from a spider.

The Side Porch

A porch hangs on the side of our house
like a child clinging to a mother's skirt.
It's covered with jumbles of stuff
that prick me when I wake at night:
bikes rusting in the weather,
a bar barbeque grill (we used once last year),
a stepladder, children's balls, a moldering broom.
And that's not all.

Homeownership accretes
manmade things that sun and wind
and rain destroy. What would it take, an hour?
to clear entropy away, to make things right
so I can sleep at night. Unless I act,
those bikes will sit there
until tires crumble to dust
and seats curl in petals to the sky.

East Glacier Lake

The moon was just coming up
over the pines below.
I fed the fire and walked down to the lake
to wash my pan and fork
and draw water for the night.
The lake was mirror smooth,
purple and orange in the dusk.

I sat by the fire and smoked.
Fatigue of the week settled on me.

Sometime in the night,
the glacier ceased melting into the lake
and woke me up.
Outside the tent, I shivered
and heard nothing but my own breathing.
The moon was out full,
setting gray-white rocks and rubble alight.

The lake looked lit from within.
Hearing nothing, I listened some more.
Ice had formed a thin skein
over the surface near the rocky shore.
My fire still glowed.

Sales Meeting, Redux

My eyes fall to slits
as I think of wife and home,
kids on the swingset and lemonade,
cool grass underfoot.

Chin propped on fist-and-elbow stilts,
I shake out of chicken pecks
but summer sunlight on the playground
is winning.

My head falls forward, eyelids close—
I've lost but won. I feel hot breeze
work my hair. I lean back,
push my feet forward;
my swing pendulums into the green.

Radio Flyer

I had a dream you bought a new wagon,
red and sleek, Radio Flyer in white
across the side.

I filled it with flowers, ran it across prairie hills,
zigzagged between bison and Indians,
and cowboys leaning on saddle horns.

I floated on pea-green rivers—
fish silhouetted in mushroom blue—
and off into the sea,

where waves sparked and shone
in shark phosphor and coral spike.

I woke, wheels a-squeak in prairie grass,
I pulled into sunset and down into a valley,
basement dark and dank.

Behind, wildflowers glowed
between the tracks of my Radio Flyer,
a map of the journey back to you.

chopping wood

axe arcs, divisions and rearrangements
across knuckled-branch anarchy—
neat, blond wedges in a wash of chaos

feathers of morning fog drift down the hill
I stop, chest heavy, reverberating
the quiet now wet, breath-laden

here's where I split and order
the difficulties of work, family,
the everyday chore of being me
in neat stacks a little at a time

day after day,
I carry the axe with me,
if not in hand, then in heart

the handle's warm, blade clean and cold,
nicks across the edge
like sparks spiraling into night

Tight Blue

She comes apart, shirt bunched
about her breasts
and showing hip going to fat—
but not yet.

She turns, skirt falls a little
reveals the elastic line
of white cotton, tag flipped up
like a baited fish hook.

She straightens everything out
with a whisk of fingers, cinches it
all tight with a snap. Nearby,
a breath turns to a sigh.

The Lover

Coffee spoons tinkle against morning,
she tells me her nightmares—
house-trapped old women,
ghosts asleep on park benches,
walkers and wheelchairs and ventilators.

She touches her cheek, wrinkles spider away,
veins creep along the back of her hand.

I listen and watch and want to remember
when I spread my fingers
across her skin, calm and smooth.

every damn day

i don't care much
whether I have a soul
or if death transforms me

i don't even care
about heaven or hell
or the in between

this poor sinner
pays penance
in doubt and self-recrimination

i seek the solace
of breezy days
in early spring

when the crocus
pushes through fallen leaves
and tells of new life

so I work,
toil purgatory days
suffer tortures of the damned

someday, i hope
to come out into sun
as the insect struggles

scratches, crawls
through the soil
up into the light of day

i'm redeemed when
i find myself free
of me

dark

I came back here to remember
our first night alone in these woods
two boys, their tent, and their pipes

honey mushroom and jack-o-lantern
shimmered, blazed a blue path
through this stretch of hardwood

campfire stroked the oak canopy
we talked of god and girls and love
click beetles skittered over glowworms in the leaves

and after, when embers had died,
foxfire cast aurora around us and railroad worms
swung like ornaments in hawthorns

night gleamed, shined, radiated
we sat and waited and watched
silver-crusted, moon-flecked, fireflied

heat lightning danced on the horizon
we dreamed of growing up
driving cars, and drinking beer

and we drank and drove
fell in with girls
and forgot this place

the quiet of it all
this vast world where you and I
believed we would live forever

the night isn't as bright as I remember
life just hasn't been the same
since you've been gone

filibuster

i've put my head in a box
to carry around
and take out when I need it

safe, under my arm,
my head in my box
thinks about dangers
heads are exposed to
out in the open

the box creates its own noise,
dims the lights,
softens the jangle,
makes my days less harsh,
easier to take or leave

i hear what you say
but many times
music fills the box
images flicker,
a new show every minute

that's about as much
as i've accomplished so far,
a warm, secure container

beyond which cruel emotion
washes against other shores

i get no safer
than when i'm not me
i suppose that's quite enough

Playhouse

He was nine.
It was a special project, father and son.

We worked all summer to build that hut.
Neighborhood kids, ladders, lots of hammers.
He played in it with his friends
until his friends didn't come anymore.

After a couple of years,
he moved on. New school. New friends.

Two grown men tore that house down
in just two and a half hours.
We marveled
at our pile of splintered wood.

I'm sorry to see it go, he said,
as the truck drove away into spring day.
At least, we built it together
and together we took it down.

Ismael Gallegos, Superman

Ismael runs the credit union at the mission;
His members driving used cars:
10 percent down, 8 percent interest,
twenty-four, thirty-six, forty-eight months,
depending on the make, model,
and blue-book value.

His desk sits small in the corner,
two chairs for customers he treats
as if they were the only ones
with cash in his care.

Unless he has a client, he flips
the sign on his door to *closed*
at precisely 5 p.m. and straightens his papers.
His Claudia welcomes him home with dinner.

Dishes cleaned and dried and put away,
kids settled in homework,
he pets the cat and sets out his jacket and tie
for the next day's business.

After sunset, he strolls his garden in the dark
and talks to his plants and trees—
like his members, they need room to grow
and a little encouragement.

All around him, neighbors' windows flicker
in television light.

Elizabeth Dobson, Oct. 7, 1903-April 3, 2001

She was 86 the day we sat in the kitchen
that smelled of ghosts, bread crumbs, and old tea.
She held the newspaper over the table,
Look at that nigger girl.
Isn't she pretty?

Spring threw bolts of green against the windows.
But the kitchen was dim, as always;
the drawers around us bulged with rubber bands,
old bolts, nuts, and screws.

That day, she put burned toast
out the kitchen door,
The birds will be happy;
they don't get much from me.

She went to the home at 88—
$60,000 in the bank
and old notes worth some more:
burnt toast-rubber band-bolt-nut-screw money.

At her funeral, Ione, 97 too,
said grandma was the prettiest,
kindest woman she ever knew,
a good friend, generous,
always devoted to others.

I cupped Ione's cheek
and remembered that newspaper photo.
We lit a candle, *a prayer to the Virgin,* Ione said.
I stared up at the ivory marble statue,
felt the soft warmth that radiated
from Ione's coffee-colored skin.

Fighting Fires

Spring again, time to clean
generations out of the corners.
We never get them all, never all,
the flakes of skin, food crumbs,
the wool turned to moth dust.

Here again is Walter Bell
who fights fires, and fights
one now down the street.

A camera crew stands out front.
Neighbors, in what will be
their only TV appearances,
say an old couple just bought it
as a fixer upper.

Behind them, in flashing blue and red light,
Walter and the other men spray water,
rake smoke from cinders.

At a safe distance, I mill around
with others and wonder
about lives lived in our houses
and where their memories have gone.

I remember it is spring again
and the only time a house is clean
is when it burns and swirls
into the wind or is smeared
on the face of a guy I went
to high school with.

to walk

bandy-legged, newspaper under arm,
skinny little paul—neighbor, friend, critic—
walks and walks and walks

he walked to the cemetery
when we buried my grandmother

his grayed beard and bushy eyebrows
flittering in the wind
he remembered her fondly
as neighbor, friend, critic

he didn't want a ride (he never does)
but said he wanted to visit
someone earthed long ago
in a distant row of stones

his mother, whom I never heard of,
his father, who disappeared,
or a sister, brother, or cousin?
he never said

he turned to the hill
that rolled down to a wooded creek
happy to see us, he said,
happy one more day
to walk

Bum

A funny little man
with a bent back and one foot—
the other lost in the *big freeze of '83*—
drinks the last of his Sterno
and breaks rock with a can of tuna.
He smells of wood smoke and burning tires.

He runs his callused fingers
through his John the Baptist wave,
and says the denim in his jeans
is greased with the handshakes he's had
since he picked those pants up
from the Salvation Army in 2010.

He's not a guy you look in the eye.
But his pockets hold cards,
tattered, faded things—
Thanksgiving and Christmas,
and at least one Father's Day—
things he mutters to you about
as semis snap the metal plates above.

Against the End of Hope, or John Stack's Last Good Try

His cohorts, once and former,
drank wine and smoked cigars,
in robes, bleary eyed, like Romans,
orgified, just in from debauch.

And inside, the Senate sent up a cheer,
a wail of laughter that busted
along the street, where we warmed our hands
under the haunches of dogs
with hardly any breath left in them.

At the door of the chapel, meanwhile,
a whole line of mouths opened
on cue of everlasting life.
At the altar, Caesar wrapped laurels
around the heads of orphans who'd done him favors.

And there was our man, the one who stood for us,
making one last try—after we had given up—
to reinstate the republic, to make us believe
in something other than flesh
and empty prayers and false gods.

Last time we saw him, he was blowing the base
of the fire, sending sparks into Cleopatra's veils
to signal gods the experiment wasn't over,
the patient's heart hadn't stopped—not yet.

The Buddha, 39th and Main

Eyes closed, breath in gentle waves,
his hands rest on knees
raised from the sidewalk
on cement-dusted boots.

In jangles of humanness, salty and ripe—
quiet panics, sudden shouts,
heat brushes off the street in puffs—
he is cool stillness.

Wrist watches gandered and tapped,
feet click pavement, shuffle in the heat—
Detached from desire, suffering ends.
The concrete is warm, the bus has come.

Tamale Lady

Tamale lady knocks at the door,
waves, smiles. On the driveway,
a paper bag steams in a two-wheeled cart,
the kind old people pull behind them.

In winter, the sweet ones, with raisins,
hot and precious in foil,
do more than the hearth for the inside of a man.
In summer she makes them with peaches
from old man Rodriquez's tree,
sunshine dripped with honey.

When her cart's empty
before she goes home to work,
she reads her little Bible
at a bus stop on the Avenida.

Tree Surgeon

Swinging from a top limb,
he dances, hops, pirouettes—
one rope width from certain incapacity
or death, depending how he falls.
He is a professional. Tools dangle from his belt.
With handsaw, then chainsaw,
he severs sucker and bough from the trunk
and tosses them in arcs to his man on the ground
A chipper chokes and screams out front.

The tree surgeon pulls himself higher
through leaves and thin air.
The neighbors gasp at his supernatural power,
wonder how a man can fly
without fear in an atmospheric layer
all his own. He sees everything
and nothing but a tree.

Earthbound again, he unbraids himself,
the tree slenderer for his work.
Out of his hardhat now, dust mask pulled below his chin,
he hefts himself up on the pile
in the back of the truck—limbs that once soared,
gave us shade, perched songbirds.
He takes his water bottle, drinks deeply,
tells us he's hungry and can't wait
to get home for dinner.

farm kid

he jerked about the hospital bed
set up in the middle of the living room,
a moth in the bottom of a porch lamp

family had become strangers,
pictures on the wall, more strangers—
a retirement party, a wedding, a grandchild's baptism,
a paper clipping with his grandchild's name

and one more picture, another stranger,
somewhat familiar — a boy, floppy ears, narrow face,
bow tie in a one-room schoolhouse

the old man's eyes, free from worry,
looked like the kid in the frame
for the first time in seventy years

Home to Roost

Bluejays, big as chickens,
pogo along the top of the fence,
dive at the cat with its eye on the nest.

The kid next door totters across the lawn,
a kitten in each hand.

When the Titans Sleep

Winds sweep over the wall on Holly Street,
whirlpool through broken windows
and down through the house,
rays of light fall through cracks—

Four Roses bottles halo their heads,
and unstruck matches teeter on fingers
creased with soot, callused and strong.
Cigarettes stick to cracked lips like messages.

Dust dunes about their shoes,
rolls into cuffs and gathers in the corners.
Their eyelids twitch, noses whistle.
Tufts of down flutter in their beards.

family photo

a suspendered boy pulls his chin high
as if for a blow — derby tipped back,
eyebrows up, shirt buttoned to the collar

but for the smile, he's lost
in chiseled and clenched faces,
cocked fists draped over ropes along the ring

a curl of smoke rises from his cigar,
his suspenders snap,
flash powder lights the room

missouri

wind from the west
sweeps in, redfire gold and lupine blue,
heavy with fragrances of soil and wheat,
urea and cow dung, combine diesel
and pickup truck smoke

out there, a boy's just run up
a prairie hill — dew heavy shoes,
grasshopper in hand spitting brown and kicking—
to witness the birth of sky

homeward again, dreaming of horizon,
he feels the wind rise,
smells prairie perfumes from highway overpasses,
watches storms curtain sunsets,
waits for thunder to shake the ground

waking, it's as if he's fallen off the edge of the world,
and swept away in dark current,
he bumps over dunes on the bottom of the river

sacrifice

a raindrop on humus
drips down through fossils
on a cave roof

it joins others in a river
that flows out of a rock seam,
pure, clear, cold

the twelve year old cups his hands
and drinks in the sweetest memory
he'll ever taste

the old man sits in the porch swing
and daydreams

landscaping

the new yard, gravel and rock
bare ground muddied in recent rain
lies fertile on the mind

for dogwood, pink and white,
a pair of redbuds either side of the drive,
a couple of lively lilacs next to the house

out back, on the hill, where the water has run
into the basement already,
there's a place for two apples,
a peach, and a fish pond

all this gardening, digging, hoeing,
mulching around roots, smacking dust and soil
from knees of jeans and crimps of skin
presupposes the pin oak, now a sapling,
draping its green curtain over it all

shade an old man
might remember he wanted to see
as he sits on a porch swing under a broken gutter
before a house long in need of paint
in the shadow of that tree

Night Terrors

Inquisitions begin the moment
the head hits the pillow.
Night breeds thoughtfulness
that day obscured
with distractions,
eddies and ripples
in the stream of life.

The judges take their places
around the perimeter,
gavels and briefs in hand,
questioning the mind
with words spoken, left unsaid,
omissions and things left undone.
Sleep, a distant dream.

The tossing, pillow adjusting
signs of bad conscience.
Promises to do better,
plans for the future,
abstractions for a new day
made, contemplated, shuffled.
Night grows in secrets.

The cacophony at the edge of dreaming
starts when the judges clatter
into their chambers
to determine the sentence.
Decisions roughing the limn,
the descent quickens,
the bottom nearing.

Inquest over the body
moves into slumber;
a moment of peace
before guilt rushes in
and insomnia pounces.
Revenant, the patient gasps
turns over, winces.

Interrogations end at dawn.
Lessons unlearned,
the day lurches forward.
The judges, silent,
maintain watch.

I Am This City

My history crushes me.
Every street corner, section, quarter, and neighborhood
tells a story of me, the story of Kansas City.

This town is in my blood. It is me. I am it,
from DJs on Prospect, across from the hospital,
where gunfire drove me to the ground
and from beneath the car
I saw the body fall to the grass,
bullet in his head,

to the corner of 62nd and Rockhill,
stout walls, stately columns, elaborate gardens,
where she pinned me against the oak,
disrobed me below the waist,
displayed our dalliance
to rush-hour traffic.

I am Midtown, drunken swaying,
I bang fists on Main Street store windows
hoping a hand might bust through,
severe an artery, and leave me laying
in a pool on the sidewalk,
self-destructed.

I am drunks rolling out of Buddies,
Davey's Uptown Ramblers Club,
Club Royal, Grand Emporium,
Dave's Stagecoach, Blaney's, Harling's,
falling out of the dim light and neon,
smoking and waiting for buses
that don't run after midnight.

I am the Uptown, where chest pushed out,
chin cocked, eyes ablaze, I pulled people
from the stage and thought I owned something
in broken-down cars, a few sticks of furniture—
things I couldn't part with—
shreds of identity.

I am the man who wears an ankle brace,
shuffling squint-eyed, purse-lipped
from storefront to storefront,
asking if there's anything for me,
a dollar or a quarter or a sandwich
or a drink.

I am the nine-story man
with only a hole for an ear
and a metal skeleton I wear over my parka
telling stories at the bus stop—
pavement, pounding hot—
about good old days
when I had a backbone.

I am the corner of 40th and McGee,
where assaults and molestations—
the noise and the men who stalked me
for the money I owed
to a bookie whose name I never knew—
drove me to insanity.

I am John O'Hara,
who upon being held up at knifepoint,
pulled a gun and robbed the robber,
a badge of honor in a city
that sleeps nearly all the time
and where a man can nap on a park bench.

I am also the Northeast,
where people work so much
they can't get their kids to school
and where the sons and daughters
of the idle rich take rents large and small
from people who can't afford televisions.

I am the Westside,
where I've climbed the ladder
out of class-D felonies
into a 1,400-square-foot house,
an unfinished basement—
a world of possibilities
where I look out the window at my kid
playing with boys and girls of every color,

a world I never knew but to which
I always thought I belonged,
immigrants and foreigners and rich and poor
together as one,
as beautiful and ragged and kept
as any city anywhere.

I am this city in its changes and generations
each lost to another in willful forgetting.
Every street corner, section, quarter, and neighborhood
tells a story of myself, stories
that would be different and same
anywhere at any time about anybody.

I am this city, its dirty corners
and wide boulevards and clean suburbs
where nothing seems to happen
except in basements and garages.

They will have to drag me out of this city
on a stretcher.

highway beautification

highway prettification's been a problem
since appius claudius cæcus
decided to move rome's legions
faster, farther, and more efficiently

in all these years—
nay, millennia—
of highway engineering,
only the romans invented
an adequate landscaping program

romans planted romans
along the shoulder of the appian way
in single-eyebrowed mausoleums
and sprawling columbaria
slaves and the grieving kept garden fresh

i imagine for us gravestones, urns,
mausoleums decorated with crosses, stars of david,
vases, crescent moons, bronze baby booties
for a hundred thousand miles of drab,
debris-beleaguered blight

i see the garlands of death behind guardrails,
along shoulders of interstate,
four- and two-lane, urban and rural highway

no need to plant, plow, mow,
to send people in orange vests
to pluck ballooned shopping bags,
sun-faded wreaths, and litter
from no-man's land

a highway beautification project
of 330 million supplicants
bowing their heads and saying prayers
at the feet of those who passed before us,
by us, for us

the retreat from al alamein

rommel knew he lost north africa
for whatever the reason: stalingrad,
montgomery, a few tanks of fuel

oh! for a few tanks of fuel

he stared at the sea as the afrika korps
sowed devil's gardens
in coral sand behind him

intricate plantings

that when they bloomed they unmade men,
and strung them on trellises of barbed wire
in neat rows like marionettes

he took a deep breath

considered the desert laid out to the sea
said a prayer to gods of his father
for his men and his country

he did not mention his boss

the field marshal knew loving gods

can't choose sides. he prayed for montgomery,
alexander, stumme, and bastico, too, and their soldiers

the fight already ended

on a hill beneath skies at tel el-eisa,
there are no sides, good or bad,
just desert and sea, scorpions and gulls

and men asleep in ossuaries, vaults full of stars

Signals

Just yesterday, Grace, my next door neighbor,
puffed into the sky, arms of her coat
like fish gills. She floated back about
Halloween orange on the horizon
and let her blue balloon puff up
the radio mast and beam into space
in shards of flashing light.

Today, Grace little-old-ladied her way
to the grocery store, then hup-hup-hupped
to the shade of an elm. Last I saw her,
somewhere between owl hungry
and Coahuila purple, she was levitating
like a trout swimming upstream, waving
to the children on the way home from school.

sales meeting

bubble-eyed buddha rests
on the bottom of a pop bottle,
he smiles at a crowd
that applauds the arrival of enlightenment

sometime this afternoon,
you can count on a flash to break the room,
make our innards spill to the floor and there,
soaked up in carpet fiber,
form miasma that will lift buddha
into heaven from that bottle of pop

and show us the light
in our faces
where it's always been

apparitions

we could smooth puddles tonight
when the temperature reaches zero
with the Zamboni in the Lona Auto parking lot—
the one in front of the mural of Don Diego
kneeling at the feet of the Virgin.

but there's not much to say
about Zamboni strayed and foundered
before the Virgin of Guadalupe
in a junk yard growling dogs guard

still, slick ice for the Virgin, Don Diego,
and us to skate tight circles on with shivering dogs
until the sun melts our little paradise
and sends us skittering back home
to sleep off our dream

now, though, in night muffle,
snow rimes the puddle,
ice crystals feather windshields,
buried in parkas, we walk

alone no more

midday heat thrusts miasmas
from the victim smiling skyward,
empty eyes gawking different directions,
rictus cocked, drooling on the yellow stripe

in tire tread
there is being, demise, vivacity, mortality;
sons daughters mothers fathers
friends acquaintances self—
mounds of earth, urns, carved stones—
damnation, salvation, ruination, redemption

the rearview mirror frames a procession,
attendants in black strut over their treasures,
peck tufts of fur from pavement.

surface tension

settled into cushions in the solarium
cat tinkling around bare feet

we read as evening falls on orchid-skirted palms
sprays of lemon blooms swathe cherubs

pages turn, breaths echo at babes' ankles

we skim the water, surface dimpled
with your breath

your skin cool
dry

out of shadow and light

on the bridge over rivers of traffic
we watched semis bustle past
in vertigo whirls

st. elmo's fire bounced along blinking skyscrapers,
masked men worked blue orbs,
showered streets in curtains of sparks

we walked on sidewalk crumbles—
fast food trash, broken concrete,
the remnants of last years shoe laces—
into windy rooms between buildings

women floated through lobbies,
men patted bellies through revolving doors,
valets raised hands, flicked wrists,
made cabs appear

then toward home and at the bridge
we stopped to watch men at the wheels of trucks,
and listened for news from abroad

Price of Success

If anyone ever asks
what it takes to make it,
just tell them it costs
one thousand and fifty dollars:

Rome, one way, one thousand dollars,
Umbria, by train, fifty bucks.

epoch

at birth,
add up all the revolutions
of all the world's wheels,
toothed gears, fans, flywheels,
clock hands, balls rolling across playgrounds,
and all other round things turning,
and multiply by two

add the number each morning,
multiply by two again, into next month,
next year, next decade

at thirty-two feet per second squared
breath becomes sight,
until near the speed of light,
you can touch silence,
taste the immobility
that at nine months or ninety years
delivers you home

Patrick Dobson is a writer, scholar, and poet. He is the author of two award-winning travel memoirs, *Seldom Seen: A Journey into the Great Plains* (2009) and *Canoeing the Great Plains: A Missouri River Summer* (May 2015). His first book of poetry, *a brief infidelity and other reveries*, was published by Spartan Press in 2017. He earned a doctorate in American History and American Literature in 2013 and teaches American History, Modern Latin American History, and Western Civilization at Johnson County Community College in Overland Park, KS.

This project was made possible, in part, by generous support from the Osage Arts Community.

Osage Arts Community provides temporary time, space and support for the creation of new artistic works in a retreat format, serving creative people of all kinds — visual artists, composers, poets, fiction and nonfiction writers. Located on a 152-acre farm in an isolated rural mountainside setting in Central Missouri and bordered by ¾ of a mile of the Gasconade River, OAC provides residencies to those working alone, as well as welcoming collaborative teams, offering living space and workspace in a country environment to emerging and mid-career artists. For more information, visit us at www.osageac.org

Osage Arts Community

www.ingramcontent.com/pod-product-compliance
Lightning Source LLC
Chambersburg PA
CBHW020125130526
44591CB00032B/528